HOW DOES SHE DO THAT, CHARLIE BROWN?

Selected cartoons from
YOU'RE WEIRD, SIR! Volume 2

They say the same of Centaurs $\overline{VII}$!
GOOD LUCK.
Hope you have only happy
memories of Twickers.

4ᵗ May 1985

D1355283

PEANUTS Comic Strips by Charles M. Schulz
Copyright © 1981 by United Feature Syndicate, Inc.

First published in the United States of
America 1984 by Ballantine Books

Coronet edition 1985

British Library C.I.P.
Schulz, Charles M.
  How does she do that, Charlie Brown? : selected
  cartoons from You're weird, Sir! volume 2.
  I. Title
  741.5'973   PN6728.P4

  ISBN 0–340–37761–5

Printed and bound in Great Britain for
Hodder and Stoughton Paperbacks, a
division of Hodder and Stoughton Ltd.,
Mill Road, Dunton Green, Sevenoaks,
Kent (Editorial Office: 47 Bedford
Square, London, WC1 3DP) by
Cox & Wyman Ltd, Reading

How does she do that, Charlie Brown?

**Selected cartoons from
YOU'RE WEIRD, SIR!
Volume 2**

Charles M. Schulz

● 1958 United Feature Syndicate, Inc.

CORONET BOOKS
Hodder and Stoughton

ALL RIGHT, LUCY, WHAT'S YOUR EXCUSE THIS TIME?

WAS IT THE SUN IN YOUR EYES? WAS IT THE FOG? THE WIND? THE MOON? THE STARS? WHAT WAS IT THIS TIME?

I THINK THERE WERE TOXIC SUBSTANCES COMING FROM MY GLOVE, AND THEY MADE ME DIZZY...

IF THERE'S A "HALL OF FAME" FOR EXCUSES, SHE'S IN!

➡

THE WORLD MAY NEED RAIN, BUT IT ALSO NEEDS BASEBALL GAMES

NO, IT DOESN'T..IT ONLY NEEDS RAIN..

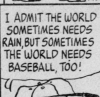

I ADMIT THE WORLD SOMETIMES NEEDS RAIN, BUT SOMETIMES THE WORLD NEEDS BASEBALL, TOO!

YOU'RE WRONG.. THE WORLD ALWAYS NEEDS RAIN...

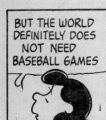

BUT THE WORLD DEFINITELY DOES NOT NEED BASEBALL GAMES

THEN WHY ARE YOU CARRYING THAT BASEBALL GLOVE?

IN CASE IT RAINS!

There are seven continents; Africa, Asia, Australia,

Europe, North America, South America and Aunt Arctica.

I'M GLAD YOU DIDN'T LEAVE HER OUT

WHAT DO YOU MEAN BY THAT?

I'LL NEVER GET A SCHOLARSHIP TO A BIG EASTERN COLLEGE WITH YOU BOTHERING ME!

HEY, EUDORA, HAVE YOU DECIDED ANYTHING YET ABOUT SUMMER CAMP?

WELL, I DON'T WANNA GO WHERE THEY SING SONGS AROUND A CAMPFIRE... THAT ALWAYS MAKES ME FEEL SAD AND LONELY...

AND I HATE PING-PONG, AND ARTS AND CRAFTS, AND HIKING AND GROUP DISCUSSIONS...

MAYBE YOU SHOULD JUST STAY HOME..

THAT'S IT!!

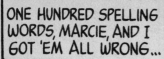

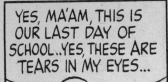

YES, MA'AM, THIS IS OUR LAST DAY OF SCHOOL..YES, THESE ARE TEARS IN MY EYES...

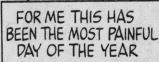

FOR ME THIS HAS BEEN THE MOST PAINFUL DAY OF THE YEAR

NO, MA'AM, I'M NOT SENTIMENTAL

I GOT MY FINGER CAUGHT IN MY BINDER!

BEAN BAGS ARE
A BOON TO
SULKERS

IF YOU'RE GOING TO SEE A WORM, YOU HAVE TO STARE AT THE GROUND

TILT YOUR HEAD A BIT AND LOOK OUT OF ONE EYE...

KLUNK!

DON'T WORRY, THE TILTING WILL COME

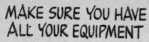

MAKE SURE YOU HAVE
ALL YOUR EQUIPMENT

AND DON'T FORGET
TO FILL YOUR CANTEEN
WITH WATER...

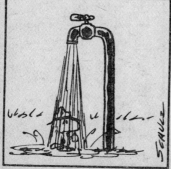

HOW DO YOU GET EVEN WITH AN OCEAN?

SIXTEEN, SEVENTEEN, EIGHTEEN, NINETEEN...

I'M GOING TO BE A FAMOUS GOLFER...

THEREFORE, IT STANDS TO REASON, LUCILLE, THAT I NEED THAT GOLF BALL MORE THAN YOU DO..

?

I'M ENTERING A KID'S GOLF TOURNAMENT NEXT WEEK, MARCIE, AND AFTER I WIN, I'LL TURN PRO...

WHAT ABOUT COLLEGE, SIR? YOU CAN'T NEGLECT YOUR EDUCATION...

I CAN ALWAYS GO TO COLLEGE, MARCIE, AFTER I'M RICH AND FAMOUS...

YOU'RE WEIRD, SIR

IF I'M GOING TO BE YOUR CADDY, SIR, I THOUGHT I SHOULD LEARN SOME GOLF EXPRESSIONS

"DRIVE FOR SHOW..PUTT FOR DOUGH"

THAT WAS GOOD, MARCIE..WHAT OTHER ONES DID YOU LEARN?

FORE!

HERE IT IS IN THE PAPER, MARCIE..WE TEE OFF AT NINE O'CLOCK MONDAY MORNING

WE'RE NOT PLAYING AT ST. ANDREWS, ARE WE, SIR?

HARDLY, MARCIE

THAT'S GOOD BECAUSE I HAVE TO BE HOME BY FIVE

WATCH THE BALL, MARCIE

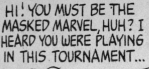

HI! YOU MUST BE THE MASKED MARVEL, HUH? I HEARD YOU WERE PLAYING IN THIS TOURNAMENT...

HE SURE LOOKS FAMILIAR, DOESN'T HE? WITH THAT MASK ON, THOUGH, I CAN'T TELL WHO IT IS...

HIS CADDY LOOKS FAMILIAR, TOO, SIR...

ALL RIGHT, I GOT A NINE ON THE FIRST HOLE..WHO'S GONNA KEEP SCORE?

LET THE MASKED MARVEL DO IT... HE HAS AN HONEST FACE...

HERE, MASKED MARVEL.. WRITE DOWN THE SCORES... WE ALL GOT NINES ON THE FIRST HOLE....

HOW DO YOU WRITE A NINE?

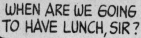

LET'S SEE.. I REMEMBER CHIPPING OVER THE GREEN... AND THEN...

HEY, MASKED MARVEL, WHAT DID I GET ON THE FOURTH HOLE? LET ME SEE THE SCORE CARD...

I THOUGHT I HAD A THREE, BUT MAYBE YOU'RE RIGHT...

AFTER THIS TOURNAMENT IS OVER, FUNNY-FACE, HOW ABOUT YOU AN' ME TAKIN' OFF SOME PLACE?

AAUGH!

HEY! MY CADDY FELL IN THE LAKE WITH ALL MY CLUBS! WHAT AM I GONNA DO?

YOU CAN'T ASK FOR ADVICE, JOE..IT'S A TWO-STROKE PENALTY!

LOOK AT THE WAY JOANNE CARNER HITS THAT GOLF BALL!

I COULD HAVE BEEN A FAMOUS PRO, TOO, MARCIE, IF YOU HADN'T THROWN MY CLUBS IN THE LAKE...

YOU HAVE LOTS OF TIME YET, SIR... WOMEN'S GOLF IS STILL ON THE UPSWING...

GOLF IS ON THE BACKSWING, MARCIE...

DON'T BE CUTE, SIR!

I WONDER IF IT'S GOING TO BE TOO HOT TO PLAY TODAY...

DON'T WORRY ABOUT THE HEAT, MANAGER..

IF YOU WEAR YOUR CAP UPSIDE DOWN, AND FILL IT WITH ICE WATER, THE HEAT WON'T BOTHER YOU A BIT!

LET'S NOT BOTHER LUCY..SHE'S SULKING

I SUPPOSE WHEN ONE MEMBER OF A FAMILY SULKS, IT AFFECTS EVERYONE IN THE FAMILY...

NO, I DON'T THINK SO..

REALLY? WHERE HAVE I FAILED?

LOOK, MARCIE, A BUTTERFLY LANDED ON MY NOSE!

YOU ARE PROBABLY ONE OF ONLY A DOZEN PEOPLE IN THE HISTORY OF THE WORLD WHO HAS HAD A BUTTERFLY LAND ON HER NOSE

DO YOU THINK IT'S AN OMEN?

NO, IT'S A BUTTERFLY ALL RIGHT

I HATE YOU, MARCIE!

WHAT'S A BUTTERFLY DOING ON MY NOSE? DO YOU THINK IT'S LOST?

I HOPE IT DOESN'T THINK IT'S FOUND A HOME...

IF IT DOES, IT PROBABLY THINKS IT'S FOUND A CONDOMINIUM!

YOU'RE A BIG HELP, MARCIE..

I'M TRYING NOT TO GIGGLE, SIR

AND THAT'S WHAT HAPPENED, CHUCK

FIRST, THE BUTTERFLY LANDED ON MY NOSE... THEN, WHILE I WAS ASLEEP, IT TURNED INTO AN ANGEL, AND FLEW AWAY!

THE BUTTERFLY CHOSE **ME**, CHUCK! DOESN'T THAT JUST MAKE YOU SHIVER ALL OVER?

I'M TRYING TO STAY HUMBLE, CHUCK...

THIS BUTTERFLY LANDED ON MY NOSE, SEE...THEN, IT SUDDENLY TURNED INTO AN ANGEL AND FLEW AWAY! MARCIE SAID SHE SAW IT!

I REALLY DIDN'T...I JUST MADE IT UP...

IT WAS A MIRACLE, LINUS!

I DON'T KNOW WHY I DID IT..

I THINK I'VE BEEN CHOSEN FOR SOME REASON!

I NEVER SHOULD HAVE SAID ANYTHING

PLAIN, SIMPLE, LITTLE OL' ME!

SCHULZ

I THINK I WAS CHOSEN TO BRING A MESSAGE TO THE WORLD, LINUS..I REALLY DO!

WHY ELSE WOULD A BUTTERFLY LAND ON MY NOSE, AND THEN TURN INTO AN ANGEL?

WELL, THE WORLD CAN CERTAINLY USE A MESSAGE

HOW ABOUT THIS?

IF THERE'S A FOUL BALL BEHIND THIRD BASE, IT'S THE SHORTSTOP'S PLAY!

YES, MA'AM, I'D LIKE TO SPEAK TO THE PREACHER, PLEASE..THE ONE I SEE ON TV ALL THE TIME...

I THOUGHT MAYBE HE'D BE INTERESTED IN A MIRACLE THAT I PERSONALLY KNOW OF..

HE'S BUSY? I'M SURE HE IS, BUT THIS WAS QUITE A MIRACLE...A BUTTERFLY LANDED ON MY NOSE, SEE, AND...

A SUNDAY SCHOOL PAPER? YES, MA'AM, I'LL TAKE IT...BUT NOW LET ME TELL YOU ABOUT THE ANGEL...

Schulz

YOU LOOK TIRED, SIR

I'M EXHAUSTED, MARCIE

I'VE BEEN TO THREE TABERNACLES, FOURTEEN CHURCHES AND TWO TEMPLES...

NO ONE WANTED TO HEAR ABOUT YOUR MIRACLE?

ALL I GOT WAS A BUNCH OF TRACTS AND THIS...

"WANT TO RECEIVE A BLESSING? DONATE TO OUR NEW LAWN SPRINKLING SYSTEM"

HELLO, JOE MOUTH? IS THIS THE JOE MOUTH TALK SHOW? WELL, I'M A FIRST-TIME CALLER, BUT A LONG-TIME LISTENER...

I'D LIKE TO TELL YOUR LISTENERS ABOUT A MIRACLE..THIS BUTTERFLY LANDED ON MY NOSE, SEE, AND...HELLO?

JOE MOUTH? HELLO? HELLO? HELLO?

SORRY, FOLKS.. JUST ANOTHER NUT CALLING IN...

I'M NOT ANOTHER NUT!!

AN ANGEL APPEARED TO ME, SCHROEDER, AND TOLD ME TO GIVE THIS MESSAGE TO THE WORLD...

"IF A FOUL BALL IS HIT BEHIND THIRD BASE, IT'S THE SHORTSTOP'S PLAY!"

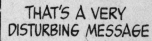

THAT'S A VERY DISTURBING MESSAGE

I EXPECT TO BE PERSECUTED...

"IF A FOUL BALL IS HIT BEHIND THIRD BASE, IT'S THE SHORTSTOP'S PLAY!"

THAT'S THE MESSAGE I FEEL THE ANGEL TOLD ME TO GIVE TO THE WORLD...

THERE ALSO MAY BE A FEW EARTHQUAKES AND SOME FLOODS

THAT'S FRIGHTENING!

THANK YOU!

I REFUSE TO BELIEVE THAT WOODSTOCK HAS DISCOVERED EVIDENCE OF THE LOST ISLAND OF ATLANTIS AT THE BOTTOM OF MY WATER DISH!

→

MAY I THINK ABOUT THAT FOR A MINUTE?

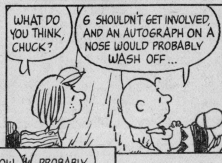

SURE, CHUCK..IN THE MEANTIME, HERE'S ANOTHER ONE....SAY A PERSON HAS KIND OF A BIG NOSE, AND ANOTHER PERSON CALLS HER "BASEBALL NOSE," AND TELLS HER NOT TO GO NEAR THE BALL PARK 'CAUSE SOMEONE MIGHT AUTOGRAPH HER NOSE, SHOULD SHE BE OFFENDED?

WHAT DO YOU THINK, CHUCK?

G SHOULDN'T GET INVOLVED, AND AN AUTOGRAPH ON A NOSE WOULD PROBABLY WASH OFF...

YOU DON'T KNOW ANYTHING ABOUT LOVE, CHUCK!

PROBABLY NOT

SCHULZ

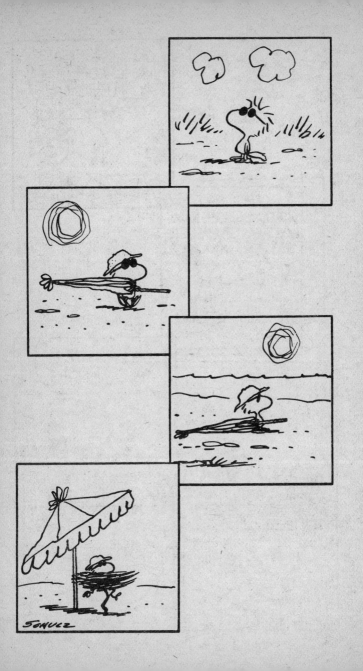

LOOK, BUG, I TOLD YOU YOU'RE IN THE WRONG PLACE...SHOW ME THOSE TICKETS...

"SECTION TEN, ROW 6..." WELL, THAT'S FINE, BUT THIS ISN'T THE COLISEUM! YOU'RE IN MY SUPPER DISH!

I DON'T CARE IF YOU DID PAY FOR YOUR PARKING!

SCHULZ

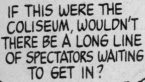

Dear Sweetheart,
I miss you
so much.

Tears of loneliness
fill my eyes as I
think of you.

Tears of love
drop onto these
lines I write.

TEARS!

YOUR STUPID BEAGLE JUST GROWLED AT ME!

I'M SURE HE DIDN'T MEAN ANYTHING BY IT...

WELL, HE DOESN'T HAVE TO BE SO BEAGLIGERENT!

I DON'T THINK YOU SHOULD BE SO HARD ON SNOOPY.. AFTER ALL, HE IS OUR WATCHDOG...

HA! SOME WATCHDOG!

WHAT COULD HE EVER DO FOR ME IF A BURGLAR GOT IN?

WELL, I GUESS THIS MIGHT HELP...

HEY, BIG BROTHER, WAKE UP!

WHAT SHOULD I DO NEXT WEEK IF THE TEACHER ASKS ME SOMETHING, AND I DON'T KNOW THE ANSWER?

JUST TELL HER YOU DON'T KNOW

CAN I USE YOUR NAME?

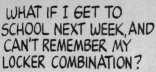

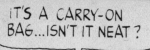

DON'T YOU EVER DO ANYTHING TO MAKE HIS DINNER LOOK NICE?

→

OH, YEAH? WELL, DOGS CAN DO LOTS OF THINGS THAT BIRDS CAN'T DO...

BIRDS CAN'T RIDE IN CARS WITH THEIR HEADS OUT THE WINDOW...

A DOG CAN STICK HIS HEAD OUT OF THE WINDOW AND LET HIS TONGUE AND EARS FLAP IN THE WIND LIKE THIS...

YOU KNOW WHAT WOULD HAPPEN IF A BIRD WAS IN A CAR, AND HE STUCK HIS HEAD OUT OF THE WINDOW?

THAT'S WHAT WOULD HAPPEN..

WHICH, NOW THAT I THINK ABOUT IT, DOESN'T PROVE VERY MUCH..

WELL, I DIDN'T WANT TO BRUSH IT AWAY BECAUSE I MIGHT HURT IT...

AFTER A WHILE I MUST HAVE DOZED OFF.. WHEN I OPENED MY EYES, THE BUTTERFLY WAS GONE!

YOU'LL NEVER GUESS WHAT HAPPENED... IT HAD TURNED INTO AN ANGEL, AND FLOWN AWAY!

HA HA HA HA HA HA HA HA

WELL, THIS WAS OBVIOUSLY A MIRACLE! I HAD BEEN CHOSEN TO BRING A MESSAGE TO THE WORLD!

WHAT WAS THIS MESSAGE I WAS TO BRING TO THE WORLD? AFTER MUCH THOUGHT, I DECIDED IT WAS THIS, "A FOUL BALL HIT BEHIND THIRD BASE IS THE SHORTSTOP'S PLAY!"

HAHAHA HA HA HA HA HA

MA'AM, IF IT'S OKAY WITH YOU, I'LL TAKE THE QUESTIONS AFTER SCHOOL OUT IN THE ALLEY BEHIND THE GYM!

This is my report on the letter M, which is the thirteenth letter of our alphabet.

OR THE TWELFTH IF THE LETTER "J" IS OMITTED

IF WHAT?

➤➤

HOW CAN I GET THE SLIVER OUT OF YOUR FINGER IF YOU WON'T LET ME NEAR YOU?

I DON'T WANT YOU POKING AROUND WITH THOSE TWEEZERS!

OKAY, WISE GUY, HOW ARE YOU GONNA GET IT OUT?

IF I SHAKE MY HAND REAL HARD, MAYBE IT'LL **FALL** OUT!

ALSO AVAILABLE FROM CORONET BOOKS

☐	04491 8	Good Ol' Snoopy (3)	£1.10
☐	04295 8	Here Comes Snoopy (6)	£1.10
☐	04405 5	All This And Snoopy, Too (11)	£1.10
☐	12786 4	We Love You, Snoopy (19)	£1.10
☐	15829 8	It's For You, Snoopy (28)	£1.10
☐	15698 8	You're Not For Real, Snoopy (30)	£1.10
☐	15696 1	You're A Pal, Snoopy (31)	£1.10
☐	17322 X	You're Something Special Snoopy (33)	£1.10
☐	18303 9	There's No-one Like You Snoopy (37)	£1.10
☐	19550 9	You've Got It Made, Snoopy (40)	£1.10
☐	19927 X	You're So Smart Snoopy (42)	£1.10
☐	20491 5	You're On Your Own Snoopy (43)	£1.10
☐	21236 5	It's All Yours Snoopy (45)	£1.10
☐	21983 1	You've Got To Be You, Snoopy (47)	£1.10
☐	22159 3	You've Come A Long Way, Snoopy (48)	£1.10
☐	22304 9	That's Life Snoopy (49)	£1.10

All these books are available at your local bookshop or newsagent, or can be ordered direct from the publisher. Just tick the titles you want and fill in the form below.

Prices and availability subject to change without notice.

CORONET BOOKS, P.O. Box 11, Falmouth, Cornwall.

Please send cheque or postal order, and allow the following for postage and packing:

U.K. – 55p for one book, plus 22p for the second book, and 14p for each additional book ordered up to a £1.75 maximum.

B.F.P.O. & EIRE – 55p for the first book, plus 22p for the second book, and 14p per copy for the next 7 books, 8p per book thereafter.

OTHER OVERSEAS CUSTOMERS – £1.00 for the first book, plus 25p per copy for each additional book.

Name ....

Address ....

....